The Millionaire Mantra

By

Stephen Christian Banner

The First Thing I See

What happens when you break through the threshold and have a peak on the other side? What happens when you look behind the curtain? When you take the step beyond the world that you know and finally find yourself in prosperity? What do you see?

Freedom

You see the world in its glorious and infinite possibilities, and this feeling, this moment, is why I have decided to write this book.

You want to move past the known world of strife and confusion and into a place that is satisfying and fulfilling.

Throughout history there have been men and women all over the world who have tapped into the kind of meditative life which brings prosperity and contentment and the hilarious thing about it is that it is free. It is free to move from a life of pressure to one of ease. From taking to giving. From asking to receiving.

And all it takes is the change of mind that comes from reflection and self-discipline. Very simple changes in your life can make a world of difference.

Before there is action there is thought. And this is the chance for you to change your thoughts so that your actions will change. The outcome will change.

Discover your own personal inner landscape and learn what it takes to become a millionaire with the millionaire mantra.

How to Begin

I have read a number of books claiming to help me in my pursuit of financial independence, but they all failed. It wasn't until I took things into my own hands (and mind) that my prosperity began to freely flow.

I studied the life habits of all of my heroes. Individuals in my own life that were happy, content, and prosperous attracted me, and I wanted to know how they came to be in this place.

The truth I found, and this is a big one, is that every single person I spoke to and researched had decided at one point or another that they would become prosperous their own way. They realized that each person has their own road to travel and that even though it is important to learn all we can from each other, it is ultimately in your hands how your life goes.

This was astonishing to me. It was a life altering change of mind. I had grown up being told that the men and women who became wealthy all followed the same path. Book after book told me that there was always one thing more to do, one similarity between all the rich people, one system, one plan, one habit, one more habit, etc.

I had been lost in the sea of self-help, until this life changing moment occurred.

It was not the system, it was me. I had to follow my own path.

So I began.

But what does it look like to begin? Well, I started with myself. I learned about mapping my own inner landscape and had to decide for myself what made me content. I had to figure out my own personal state of being, so that I could be intentional about changing it.

Beginning on this journey was one of the most frustrating moments of my life, but also incredibly rewarding. I became open to myself for the first time. I had lived and learned and grown and worked, and when I stopped to examine it all, it was like I realized that I was searching for so much that I already had.

Everyone's journey is unique, but for my own journey from owing $15,000 dollars in credit card debt, and sleeping in the basement of a relative's house at 22, to making as much as 25% growth a week in the stock market and being able to pay for all the things I wanted, was like a waterfall from the moment I began to practice the Millionaire Mantra.

What is it?

I began meditating when I was about twenty-four years old, and my outlook began to instantly change. Radically. I began to think in ways I didn't know where possible. Sometimes I would tell others that it feels like thinking in reverse.

Before we get much further along I would like to share with you what it is I say consistently as my own personal Millionaire Mantra. But it is important to note, and something I tell almost everyone I speak to, it is important to form your own mantra. It must be completely personal, so personal that it is a secret.

"Life and Love, I will be a participant today. I will live from abundance and give."

That's it. And it has changed my life.

I think it is important to clarify, that the journey to find my personal Millionaire Mantra was over a few years and struggling through a variety of options. The journey is ultimately yours, but affirming your own stance on your prosperity and continuously being mindful about that stance and about your place in the world is invaluable.

There has been story after story about great leaders, business people, and many of the world's most influential people talking about their own personal life of meditation and self-affirmation. It is possibly the one great thing that distinguishes the prosperous from the poor.

How and When should I say my mantra?

I find that the quiet of the morning has become my time for self-affirmation. I repeat my mantra to myself throughout the day, but I a most clear about my intentions for the day when I begin with this habit.

It sets me up for success.

Again, each of us is different, I know some who have their meditative time in the evening after a full day of work, and this is fine. It is important to reconnect daily to who you are becoming and the ideals that set you apart.

The strength that comes from a daily private moment with your own personal Millionare Mantra can make all the difference between confidence and self-doubt.

Seven Steps to Achieving Success

First comes clarity. First we see things clearly.

Our first step is to understand ourselves!

So how do we change our mindset about success? How do we begin to build wealth when we and those around us suffer from feeling entitled and have ingrown difficulties with commitment and the vast world of possibility?

Let's start with deciding what you want.

What is it you want to say with your life? You only have so much time here, what do you want to do with it?

Do you want to travel and experience the world? Do you want to have time to spend with your family? Do you want to be able to help those around you? Do you wish to run your own company?

What are the things that really give you joy?

Write these things down in a notebook. Look at them. Read them. See them for what they are. Meditate upon what they really say about you.

Self-reflection is a difficult task for many of us. Sometimes what we find is unpleasant, (I'm not really like that, am I?) but it is essential for finding our path to success.

There are many personality tests out there, and many self-evaluation work books. Anything that gets you closer to understanding yourself and your place in the world will help guide you toward success.

If you do not want to find a personality test, or spend money on an analyst, here are eight questions to get you started:

How do I use my free time?

Do I prefer to work alone or in a team?

Do you charge ahead or sit back and wait?

Do you worry about the future?

Are you generally organized or disorganized when it comes to work?

Do you consider how to improve yourself?

Do you take charge or sit back and let others lead?

Do you consider yourself a happy person?

Don't stop with these questions, they can launch you into a better understanding of yourself if you put in the thought and effort to do so. Understanding yourself is a step I find most often neglected and one which, when overlooked, can lead to unrealized dreams and potential. It is important to honestly and thoughtfully consider the type of person you are in order to aim for the person you want to become.

Second, we must see clearly the world around us.

This may seem an easy step, but the truth is that many entrepreneurs fail because they do not understand the world around them. You might have a great idea for a pair of sneakers that can keep your coffee warm, but if the world around you has no need or desire for this item than you will only end up spinning your wheels

Observation is the key to this step. And although most people consider themselves very observant few people really know how to see the world around them clearly.

It is important, first to know yourself in such a way that you can be intentional when observing.

Being intentional with your observations can shift your focus from a general and mostly unhelpful kind of attention to something helpful and intense.

If, for instance, you notice within yourself a strong need for the company of others, this can give you a clue into the way you can observe others and the world around you. What does this need in you do to the people around you? What does this need do in other people? Social media is a powerful entity which may have risen out of this very basic need.

Someone saw the need for connection. With a little ingenuity social media has become a colossal force in our world.

What do you notice within yourself? What do you notice when you take it into account while observing the world around you?

It sounds more complicated than it is. But it is harder than it seems. How can you focus your attention on the right things?

Successful companies often begin with a basic need sprouting from one idea and interacting with the larger world. If you keep your idea secluded it cannot grow into what it might be.

If you keep your idea alone it will only die.

Mary and Daryl both had wonderful ideas to provide breakfast delivery to early morning shift workers at a few local businesses. They both began looking into purchasing a food truck.

Mary let her idea out into the world and began observing other similar companies and speaking to people who worked these shifts. She soon found out that the smarter choice would probably be to deliver bulk orders instead of driving around in one truck to each business.

Daryl bought his truck and soon found out that most people wanted their food at the same time and he only had time for one location each morning.

Look and listen to the world around you.

My grandfather and his brothers looked at the world around them and saw opportunity. They saw a place to help, a need to fill, and they worked diligently to make their dreams turn into realities.

The stream they were given soon turned into a huge river. They were successful because they were observant and listened to their world.

Third, what endeavor or investment brings me closer to my goals?

If you go through the process of understanding yourself and your world, this may lead to a variety of options for you. Let's say you have expertise in sustainability, if you've narrowed down some of your options your list of possible endeavors to reach your goals may look like this:

Possible new Streams:

Start a weekend class or seminar series on becoming more sustainable.

Start a consulting firm that works with companies in developing 'green' programs.

Hire a ghost writer and author a book on the laws and regulations particular to this field.

Find and invest in projects that are progressing in this field.

The truth is that your list may look any number of ways with any number of options. I like to have twenty options before I even start narrowing it down.

But once you have some ideas as to your next stream, it is important to assess them within the context of your eventual goals.

Which of these moves me in the direction of my goals at the pace I wish?

Which of these endeavors has the right amount of risk for my personal plan?

Taking your success from a small stream to a powerful river is a delicate process, and the main idea is that you do not discard a stream in search of another. This is called stream hopping and gets us nowhere fast.

We've all seen someone who enjoys stream hopping. They are the entrepreneur that never gets his feet on solid ground. Nothing ever works out for him. This is not what we want. We want to add to our stream, and only discard a stream, or allow it to dry up, when it is no longer worth keeping. When it no longer adds to the river, but turns around and takes from it.

When a stream turns it may be because it is pulling all of your energy away from other stream, it may be a drain on any number of resources. When it becomes a burden then it's time to look closely at why you still have it. It is important to note the difference between a stream which is merely hard work, and one which is actually pulls resources away from your river.

Having read and reread your list of possibilities, it comes down to choosing the right one.

Here are a few questions to assist you:

Does this new stream help me toward my goal?

How does it compare to the other options?

Will it be a temporary drain on resources?

Will it improve my life?

Does the new project get me excited?

Does this new stream require preparation?

How would I begin and when would I see its completion?

Fourth, assess the investment or endeavor closely.

It is important to both use the momentum and excitement brought by something new and to also be careful and cautious when starting out.

To lean to heavily in either direction can mean disaster. So, how do you walk down the middle of the road?

Many people get discouraged when they have to do the hard work of researching a new stream, but this is where the real separation happens.

Anyone can get excited about something new. We learned how to do that at every childhood Christmas or birthday, but when we are adults the packaging and wrapping simply become more difficult to tear.

But it is here where we find out what we are made of.

The difference between the successful and the unsuccessful is almost always found at this step.

Will I stay the course? Is it worth digging when I'm not certain of what I will find?

When hard work comes into the picture, especially to those of us inundated with messages of entitlement, our doubts flood in.

There are so many hindrances in the world around us, why do we add on to them ourselves. Here are some common inner voices:

"Why would you even try?"

"This is way too difficult, and you are not equipped for this."

"You can't do it."

But this is not the truth. You can do it! If you followed the steps and find a new stream that only needs now to be thoroughly analyzed, then get to it. This is the time to work. Get moving. Do all the research needed. Understand the endeavor as best you can. Read, fill out forms, and speak to others, whatever it takes.

Yes, it can be scary, but your goals are worth the effort.

Fifth, How do I get from here to there?

After coming to a place where you understand the endeavor in a realistic way, and you've done the homework, how is it that you get from the knowledge to the digging?

How to I take a place that was not a stream and make one?

Each project is different, and therefore I espouse a rule of listening when putting my shovel into new ground.

Listen. Listen very carefully.

When I was young, my grandfather took me into the woods to bird watch. He loved birdwatching. He took me to his favorite spot next to a large brook and we sat on a log.

We listened for a very long time, and then my grandfather asked me if I heard anything. I said I didn't hear anything. And then he told me to listen first for the rhythm of the forest. The wind in the leaves and the creaking of the branches above. Then he told me to try and listen for anything outside of that rhythm.

I heard it. I heard a deer walking through the forest across the brook. Then I heard a bee next to me, and after that I heard the warbling of one of my grandfather's favorite birds. He smiled at me, and pointed to the bird high in the canopy.

This was his goal. He loved seeing this bird. And he got it by listening.

Listen first and always.

And so, this has become a mantra for me and my business. It is essential to listen carefully as you move forward.

How do I get from that first shovel full to a new and exciting stream that adds definitively to my river? I listen.

With each new task I listen. Asking these questions with each new task will be helpful:

Does this task help or hinder the over-all project?

How does this task affect my ability to see clearly the rest of the project?

Will I be wasting time if I concentrate on this task alone?

Sixth, Commitment

In an age where we all feel entitled to happiness and prosperity nothing comes harder than commitment. We practice each day the art of noncommittal language and activity.

So how do we set ourselves on the path to success when we might feel that it is our right or privilege? It is about changing our mindset, our view on the situation.

If you really and truly wish to be successful and turn your stream in to a river, than you will think thoroughly through the implications of your choices and actions.

Seeing clearly what it is you actually do with your time will help you better understand where your priorities settle.

When you have come to a better understanding of how you use your time it is then important to determine which activities get in the way of your success and which help you move forward.

It is important to be honest about every part of your life. Your work life may seem the place to look for positive actions, and home life and leisure time might be areas you think can have a negative effect. But the opposite can easily be true.

Once you have decided which activities and actions that come in the way of your success than it is your responsibility to remove them as best you can.

Real commitment takes courage.

To commit to anything is difficult, and especially something as difficult as personal success, but it is essential to stand firm and see clearly your goals so that you can take the necessary actions to achieve them.

Be hard on yourself. It may help to think of yourself as the best employee you have in your company, but he is being influenced by the worst employee of your company. You have to separate them. Be intentional about turning your bad habits into good ones.

Procrastination plagues the bad employees work, but the good employee does not want to procrastinate. If you spend time encouraging the good employee, by making schedules, appointments, deadlines, with healthy doses of leisure, than the good employee can take over, while the bad one begins to fade.

Your bad employee wishes to spend money frivolously, but if you set up a system whereby this is impossible, than the good employee can save and be frugal.

However you choose to think about commitment and the changes that need to be made that will allow you to commit is not the important part. If you truly want to turn your stream into a river, than you have to take the necessary steps.

Making it easier to commit by changing actions, environments, habits, etc., will turn the tasks you have scheduled for yourself within a day or a week more pleasurable and easier to accomplish. With each success, it may become easier.

Often the first few shovels of dirt are the most difficult.

Earlier, we talked about the seven steps toward commitment. Review them, and infuse them into your personal pursuits and vision.

Seventh, Be giving.

This is a step which has guided much of my own journey. As always, the advice of generosity seems counterintuitive in some respects to what your goal is.

But being generous can change your life in ways you didn't know where possibly. Generosity adds to your success in ways that nothing else can.

Imagine you have a stream. You wish to turn this stream into a river. And so, you go about the tasks and actions which will add new streams. New streams begin here and there.

But when the chance arises you refuse to let that water do anything more than run through your own streams.

Soon, the forest that was once a beautiful part of the landscape around you has begun to wither. You build concrete barriers to keep in every bit of water.

Soon, there is no vegetation in the forest, and the ground dries and becomes a desert.

Where will you get your water from? Do you want to live in a desert?

The beauty of living life with others and sharing in our triumphs and our failures is often what our success has really been about in the first place.

Although commitment is essential, it is important to remember why we wished success in the first place.

Go.

5 Steps Self-Confidence

We all want to be confident. We want to feel self-assured and respected. We desire the willingness and freedom to grow and change into what we know we can be.

Confidence is one of the most sought after characteristics in our world, people scramble to find it everyday. We tell ourselves we have it when we do not, we feel discouraged that we are missing it even when we do have it.

The path to self-confidence begins with a better understanding of where we are in life.

Step 1

Know Thyself

It has been said throughout history that understanding yourself is the key to many things. Many of the things we want out of life, success, happiness, fulfillment, these have all been linked to knowing ourselves. But how do we do this? How can we know ourselves? It is a great beginning to even ask the question. Asking this question does much on the way to understanding ourselves better. There are two key ways of understanding ourselves: The Large Picture Self and the Small Picture Self. The Large Picture Self is how we connect to the larger world. Understanding our place in the grand scheme of the universe, and how we connect to this larger picture. This is our place, our time, our social standing, our philosophy, etc. It is those things that connect us to the larger world.

The Small Picture Self is the self we deal with primarily as it connects to immediate stimulus; what we choose for breakfast, and how we spoke to our boss, etc. This smaller picture self allows us the only true test of ourselves as it relates to the world around us, but through this Small Picture we must seek to see ourselves with the Large Picture.

Both are essential and the way that we connect them together can put us on the path to a clearer picture of ourselves, and ultimately to a more confident demeanor.

Step 2

Know Your Goals

If you have sat down and worked out what it is you want from your life, and what it is you wish to say with the time you have here, then the drive that moves you forward will often bring with it a certain assurance about the unknown. Even if you do not know for certain what will happen tomorrow, as no one does, you at least have some direction and plan. Without knowing it you have put yourself in the position of self-confidence, and your purpose shows.

Step 3

Be Thoughtful

Many courses made with the intention to teach us all how to achieve our goals often forget the importance of a clear thought life. It is certainly important that we act on our desires, that we pursue our dreams, but without the guide of wisdom and rational thought, our desires can be distorted and often molded by others. The advertising industry will hand you the guide to success every day with a new price tag, but if you are careful and thoughtful about what it is you truly want then your energies and efforts will not be spent on someone else's goals.

Step 4

Be Active

We are not as separated as we might think, our minds and bodies coexist together as one entity and what we do with our bodies can greatly impact our mental life. Taking our bodies seriously as a part of our overall success, we can pursue our goals and our dreams as one person, rather than just mentally. Remaining physically active throughout the day can sometimes prove difficult, but with the added energy we can become the kind of self confident people we want to be.

Step 5

Give

When we set our lives on the path to success we often think of it as a series of "gettings" or "acquirings", but the truth is that real success is often deeply connected to the art of giving yourself. Giving is often the very thing which separates the successful from the unsuccessful, the fulfilled and the unfulfilled, the happy and the unhappy. When you allow yourself to be open to the needs of those around you, and you give with no strings attached, the confidence and love that is shared well outweighs the gift of the moment. We separate ourselves from the grinding gears of progress and desire and we stand along side our fellows with charity.

Creating Space for Success

5 Steps toward Positive Change

One of the greatest challenges to finding personal success is finding the space for change. Change is essential in life, and either we choose how we change or change will happen without our input. And we want to have input.

So, how do we make space for true change in our lives? How do clear away the clutter and be purposeful and intentional? Ultimately it is up to you to understand how you personally work toward your goals, but here are the five steps that have helped many people create space for success.

1. Be honest with yourself? When you define what your personal goals are, you must be honest with yourself about how these goals can be accomplished. If you are not honest with yourself about your goals, how do you know which way to go, and which changes to make?

2. Organize. Your personal and communal spaces directly effect how productive you can be. When your physical world is chaotic and unruly, it has an impact on your inner life. For some this organization becomes the goal itself, but we must be watchful and remember what our goals really are. For others, organization is a bad word and excuses come quite easily, disguising the simple laziness they excuse, when the task of organizing comes up. Be confident about your choices, and turn your physical space into one that can be productive and positive.

3. Create a daily action list. Putting your goals on paper can create the kind of space that allows for major steps toward success. Each item checked off the list is itself a success and we should treat it that way. Even if the list is deviated from, and it often is, the list acts as a guidepost for the direction we should be moving in. You may take a few different steps today, you may wander from the trail for a moment, but the list is there to help you get back on course.

4. Remove negativity. One of the most difficult things a person has to do in their life is remove the negativity. Why? I don't know, it just is. It seeps in through all the cracks and seems like a never ending battle. Our own thoughts, our friends, what we watch and read, what we hear, what we see, so many parts of our daily lives are soaked with negativity. This is why it is important to fight. It is important to be intentional about ridding your life of negativity. Being positive doesn't mean living in an imaginary world, it means realizing that the world is full of both positive and negative and seeing that what helps us in the long run to see things more clearly, and give more cheerfully, and love more deeply, and succeed more often is an attitude which reflects that positivity.

5. Help others achieve their goals. Another difficult thing to do is to see others successes as part of our own. We can be happy for others' successes just as we would be happy for our own. When we can put aside the silly competitive nature and simply be happy for those around us, we start to see our own successes more objectively and can be happier for them as well. Giving of ourselves is not an easy thing to do, but it changes our perspective and moves us more freely in the direction we want to go.

The Seven Laws of Adaptability

Law 1

Be a Listener

We are losing the art of listening. We have taken ourselves out of the stream of communication and turned off our ear. The world around us is replete with wonderful and helpful things to tell us, but we don't listen.

This is the first law of adaptability. You must learn what it means to listen. Anyone can hear, anyone can witness, but to truly listen is to attempt to understand and this is important.

In your personal journey toward success, you must take away the distraction of your own inner voice and the voices that call your attention every minute of your day and you must practice the art of listening.

Let us consider the entrepreneur who has lost the art of listening:

Mark has his goal list, he has capital, he has his winning idea and the avenues to sell. He proceeds down his path, but along the way there are signs. There are voices from those he wishes to sell his idea to. Those voices are actually pretty loud. They are engaged in his field of work and engaged with his particular product or service, and they have wisdom to offer.

Mark does not hear them. He has his own way of proceeding and he is sure it will work. He has learned about being committed from books and blogs and he has become completely committed to his own idea and the success he desires.

Mark's idea falters and ultimately fails.

Let us consider another entrepreneur who has also lost the art of listening:

Ellen has her goal list, she has capital, and her amazing idea with avenues to sell this idea. She begins down the path, but along the way there are new voices. Voices of concern. Although she has lost the art of listening she realizes that this art may ultimately be the key to preventing a failure.

And so she begins to practice. She listens to the voices around her and realizes that what sounds like criticism is often an opportunity to correct her course. Not all the voices have her best interest at heart, but as she listens she starts to understand those voices she can trust and those that she can let go.

Ellen's idea flourishes and she makes a stream of income that adds to her ultimately life goals.

So, how do we practice the art of listening?

First it is important to know where you are at. If you are a listener who struggles, then perhaps you limit your listening time. You find the optimum time for your own attention and you schedule around this. This way you can also see your progress as you become a better listener.

After this it is simply a matter of your own journey. Take moments out of your day for quiet and for solitude. Make lists of things you heard during your day.

Take time in a hectic moment to learn to hear things you would naturally dismiss.

As a child we listened like there was nothing else more enjoyable. We had a sense of wonder that guided our curiosity. Regaining this can mean the difference between failure and success. We can become adaptable in our lives to the ever-changing world around us when we first learn to listen.

Law 2

Know Your Goals

If you haven't already, take out a sheet of paper and write down a few of your long term goals and a few of your short term goals. This is a guide. Writing these things down helps you to see them clearly. And ultimately when we see our goals clearly, we can understand them better, achieve them faster, and if needs be, we can adjust them according to our newly found adaptability.

This is the beginning of any worthwhile journey. The destination! What is it you want from your life? What is it you want from the rest of this week?

It is essential to make clear decisions about what you want.

So, how does knowing your goals make you more adaptable? It is simple.

Let us say that you are an artist. Your goal is to paint a portrait of a patron of yours. This is a worthy goal and worthy of attention. You have the person sit for you and you begin to paint, but as the painting moves along, the sun shifts in the sky and the person you see in front of you is lit very different than the one you are painting.

What is to be done? You have a goal, but now the pressures from outside have changed. The impression you see now is different than the one hours ago. But if you have a clear vision of your goal, than making the adjustments in your mind to account for the new lighting is easy.

Let us say you are an entrepreneur and have just started a new business delivering coffee to people on the street. They call your service and they are delivered coffee as they walk to work or to a meeting. It is a great idea, but suddenly after a week of being open for business sales begin to fall off, and soon you have no customers.

Your goal is still the same, but suddenly something isn't working. After inquiries you find that your favorite employee is not what he professes himself to be and because you see your goals clearly, it is easy to find another partner to work with.

These are extreme examples of the kind of adaptability that creates success, but they express in a simple way what it means to have a clear goal and how easy it is to adjust your tactics when the end is clearly defined.

Law 3

The Art of Acceptance

Our inner motivations and pressures can talk a pretty big talk. Especially when we are alone. But if we learn to see our inner life as only one part of many, we can begin the journey to adaptability.

A partner to this idea is our ability to accept the constant newness of life. Whether the coming circumstance seems negative or positive, we must overcome our need for permanence so that we can learn to accept.

This is not the art of accepting bad things that you have the opportunity to change, that is laziness in the disguise of acceptance and it is an easy trap to fall into. If you choose to accept something negative even though you have the power to change it that is not the art of acceptance, that is cowardice, and laziness.

To truly learn the art of accepting we have to think about our smallest actions. In our smallest actions we build the road to success or failure. Our success is not made of one enormous action taken at the end of a long journey. It is truly every step we take on the journey toward our goals. Every single step is what we are made of. And so we must be careful about the small things.

And so we begin with our daily lives. The minutiae of life. Do we accept those things in life that we have no control over? Do we learn to accept the decisions of others, even when they don't suit us?

These may seem like things we all learned as children, but it is surprising how many adults, who have the means and ability to reach their goals, act each day like children in all their tiny moments. These tiny moments build into a life of unacceptance and failure.

So, how do we decide what to accept and what not to accept?

Simply put, we do not accept those things which are negative and that we have some power to change. But most things are not this way. Most things we do not accept are but nuisances, or even positives we haven't fully understood yet.

The outcome of not accepting these things are often the same. Arguing with no goal in mind, complaining with no goal in mind, or gossiping with no goal in mind.

The art of acceptance is learned in the small things. If we cannot learn to accept our neighbors and friends, and learn to accept what life gives to us, then how can we begin to practice the art of acceptance in our business and financial life.

The art of acceptance can help us overcome the common mistake of making poor choices when our emotions have taken the wheel. We can learn to pause, think of our goals, and take back control moving toward our success again.

Law 4

Stop Adapting

Once you've learned about the first three laws of adaptability it is important to realize what areas of life you are adapting in too much or for the sake of ease and stop adapting.

The best way to do this is to relabel your actions, by calling them what they are: appeasements, concessions, pacifications. The kind of adapting that forgets about the inner pressures, the personal motivations and desires, and gives way because of some fear.

This is not the art of accepting and it is not adapting, it is only pretending to be.

If you can change something for the better, do it!

Adaption can be the sign of a healthy mature individual, but the other side of the coin can show a selfish, proud, constantly changing person who is clearly only out for their own interests.

To move away from this danger, it is important to think of yourself as just as valuable as anyone else. Just! The value of any human life does not outweigh the value of another. Who ae you to say you are more or less valuable than someone else? You do not get to assign the value, it is already set.

When you see your own successes and failures as you would a friends and can rejoice and reflect as you would with a partner you are on the right track. You can be adaptable without leaning in either direction. Adapting out of lack of personal value or out of an inflated sense of self-worth are both recipes for disaster.

Learn to stop adapting, so you can adapt with wisdom.

Law 5

Take Small Steps Always

The truth is that there is no other way to live life. Small steps are what make up all the large ones. So learn to take small and intentional steps.

When planning your yearly budget (another place where wise adaptability comes in handy), it is important to see the ultimate goals very clearly, but to understand that the only way to achieve the kind of personal success you want you must be willing to take all the small steps to get there.

Every day is a new opportunity to practice our skills at becoming adaptable. We can take small steps every day toward our goals, and when we take each small step we can find confidence in the small successes that come.

A person with a specific personal financial goal for the year is wise to take each day as it comes. Some days add financial strain and pressures that were unexpected, and the ability to adapt can be crucial to their overall well-being.

Being intentional each day opens up the possibility to adapt and make moves toward a goal that were not expected. This is what makes many great entrepreneurs successful, the ability to adapt when it counts. To make the tiny adjustments along the road.

If you focus is only on the prize at the end, you miss out on life. Life is made up of so many wonderful experiences, both failures and successes are a part of our journey and each day we can learn to move forward or we can merely wait the day out.

Law 6

Live From Abundance

Perhaps one of the most important laws of any success story is that of living from abundance. No, this doesn't mean living beyond your means, it doesn't mean pretending to have abundance or believing so hard that it miraculously appears.

It means that abundance can be a way of life. We are all blessed with our own personal set of gifts and abilities. And we have many things to offer the world. If we hold them back until the right time, the time may never come.

We must push ourselves to live our life from abundance. We must allow ourselves to become full and overflowing. What this means is different for each person.

Personally, I believe joy is the greatest gift I can offer the world around me. I have found joy in my life so many times and in so many ways that I see it now as a part of what I can give to the world.

But I had to learn how to become abundant, how to overflow. I have a set of personal disciplines that I have gained from years of experimentation with joy. And this is one of the things I offer to the world around me: joy.

Others I know have wisdom in abundance and they have learned to live from that abundance and share themselves with the world.

Others still have been consistently blessed with financial abundance all their lives and have learned to live from that place offering what they have to the world around them. I know some who have personal strength that they offer in abundance to the world around them and their strength has been a guide for their personal success and journey.

But it is simple, if you do not have, you cannot give. But we all have, it is simply a matter of realizing what it is we have, and offering that to the world around us. Start with those closest to you. Offer your abundance to them. You will be surprised.

Law 7

See the Big Picture

Although each step is important, and being specific and intentional about our daily lives is of the utmost importance, what does it all mean if we do not have a bigger picture in mind?

The grand scheme, the goal, the success, the achievement, what we understand as the context of our lives, these are the bigger picture. These are the things which guide all of those small steps in the right direction.

We may envision our success and happiness from the dreams of someone else and because of this we have borrowed our worldview. This can only result in a vague picture, a very large, but very vague ultimate picture.

Our big picture must be personal.

What do we want from our lives? What do we wish to say with our lives? These are the questions that give us the big picture which ultimately guides our steps.

We already have a big picture from somewhere, and many of us have had to unlearn the old picture and relearn a new one. We had to do away with many preconceptions which blinded us to the truth of everyday life.

If we do not do this, if our picture is not our own, we will lose out on what life really offers us. We will have borrowed happiness and borrowed sadness and borrowed money and borrowed success.

But if we were to have someone else's goals then we would have been someone else. But we are not.

Finding Your Millionaire Mantra

Each of us is on a different journey, and what we have in mind for our lives differs from person to person. At the heart of our desires there may be fundamental similarities, but our individual lives and sense of the world are vastly different than the person sitting next to me in a restaurant or on the subway.

What does success mean to me?

It doesn't have to be illusive if we know where and how to look.

If we haven't thought about what it means for us to be successful in our endeavors and our lives, then we most likely still have an idea somewhere inside us. But sadly, if we haven't thought it through than our idea is most likely vague and filled with uncertainty.

Our ideas about certain concepts are built up over time through what we hear and see and experience and if we are not careful our concept of success may simply be an amalgamation of the dreams and wishes of others. Or worse still, if we are not intentional about what we want from our lives, our idea of success is subject to the constant barrage of advertisements and media we see every day. And those can be very intentional. The companies behind the advertisements we see know exactly the definition of success that they want you to believe.

So, how do we clear away the rubble of false ideas and borrowed intentions. Before we can unlearn what we think we know, it is wise to decide what we want to put in its place. What is the idea of success that we want to work from as we move through our lives?

What does success mean to me?

Question 1

What makes me come alive? We have all that feeling, that rush of energy that pulls us up and forward into the fray. This thing that moves you, that motivates you in a way that nothing else does, what is that?

Question 2

If I did not have to worry about finances, what would I do with my life? Whatever your answer is, there lies a key to understanding what success means to you. We may have started out saying "Money!" "To Be Famous!" but when we start to pull back the curtain we begin to see who you really are. This question isn't a magical one, it isn't a genie in a bottle, it just takes away the major concern of most people. Our concern over money is almost always at the root of what is standing in the way of true fulfillment and success.

Question 3

What would make you happy? Although happiness isn't everything it is a great guide to understanding ourselves. The things that bring us true joy and happiness are connected to us in a deep way.

Question 4

How can I offer to the world? A question that can stump even the most generous of people. What we offer to the world around us, is part of what makes us significant and special. We all can play a part in the growth and well-being of those we come in contact with. What do you offer to the world?

Starting with this basic knowledge about who we are as individuals we can move out into understanding what success truly means to us personally.

And this is the basis for your personal Millionaire Mantra. If it isn't personal, then it might as well be spoken by someone else. Think outside the box and be creative, but above all make it personal!

The Millionaire Mantra

The success I have seen from instituting a Millionaire Mantra into my own life has been astounding. And I have watched this success spill over into the lives of those around me and I have seen the idea spread like wildfire.

To take specific action in our own live, to affirm, to uplift our spirits daily, this is the intention of the Millionaire Mantra. The world is plentiful enough to allow for all of us to be fulfilled, content, and prosperous.

Take the challenge and work to find your own personal Millionaire Mantra and change your life forever. It changed me forever and I hope it does the same for you.

www.ingramcontent.com/pod-product-compliance
Lightning Source LLC
Chambersburg PA
CBHW072312200526
45168CB00014B/1411